The Forward Book
of Poetry 1995

FORWARD PUBLISHING
LONDON

First published in Great Britain by
Forward Publishing • 5 Great Pulteney Street • London W1R 3DF
in association with
Faber and Faber • 3 Queen Square • London WC1N 3AU

ISBN 0 571 17417 5 (paperback)

Compilation copyright © Forward Publishing 1994
For copyright on individual poems see acknowledgements page 7
Foreword copyright © Cressida Connolly 1994
Front cover illustration: silkscreen original by Pete Nevin

Typesetting by Graphic Ideas
Karen House • 1-11 Baches Street • London N1 6DL

Printed by Redwood Books Ltd.
Kennet House • Kennet Way • Trowbridge • Wilts. BA14 8RN

A CIP catalogue reference for this book
is available at the British Library.

To F.A.S.

Preface

POETRY IS EXPERIENCING a renaissance. These are not just my words but those of numerous journalists, critics, broadcasters and publishers. And those who love poetry are certainly not going to argue about it, for there seems every indication that the art of writing and reading poetry is very much back on the cultural agenda. In a world where alienation and loneliness thrive, the sense of being in a dialogue with another intelligence can give readers of poetry the complicity of a language of shared experience unavailable in other art forms.

This year's Forward Book of Poetry is published on October 6th 1994, Britain and Ireland's first National Poetry Day. While this anthology is designed to give readers an introduction to some of the best poetry being written today, National Poetry Day aims to remove the embarassment some people feel about reading poetry aloud. Throughout Britain and Ireland readings and poetic events are taking place in schools, bookshops, theatres, workplaces and public spaces to celebrate the day.

This collection contains the 67 poems comprising the best entries to the Forward Poetry Prizes. In the two main categories, Best Collection and Best First Collection, the judges have selected two poems from each of the five short-listed candidates. The winners of these prizes will be announced on publication day.

Once again I would like to thank our co-sponsors, John Mitchinson at Waterstone's and Jeffery Tolman at Tolman Cunard. I would also like to thank the Arts Councils of England, Scotland, Wales, Northern Ireland and Ireland, The Book Trust, the Poetry Societies of Britain and Ireland, and all the many helpers at Forward and around the country who have made this prize, this anthology and National Poetry Day possible. Finally an enormous vote of thanks to five hard-working judges who put many weeks work into sifting through the poems of the year to make their selection.

William Sieghart

Foreword

THIS IS THE third Forward Book of Poetry. As ever, it was selected by the judges of the year's Forward Prizes; this time these were Alexandra Shulman, John Gross, Carol Ann Duffy (who won the best collection prize last year), myself and Jean Binta Breeze. We sifted through more than a 140 collections, as well as more than 120 individual poems, in order to compile this book. Almost all the entries were of a high standard, which made the task of exclusion difficult, but also ensured that the final choice represented the very best poetry being published in Britain at the moment.

All of art is a kind of alchemy. Perhaps poetry is the most magical of all forms, because it can transform into gold that most everyday and overworked of materials, our common language. The same tarnished words which we employ to buy groceries, to trot out our wants and woes, or to talk about the weather can light up and glow when they are rearranged into poetry. And selecting an anthology is like panning for gold; every so often something shines out from the rest, and you know it's the real thing. This was evident from the surprising degree of consensus between we judges. Time and again one of us would nominate a collection we had enjoyed, only to find the others had earmarked the same poet, and very often the same poem too. Of course there was a certain amount of harmonious discord as well. Occasionally one of us would propose a poem with a passion which mystified the others, and after re-appraisal, these tended to fall by the way. So this is not an eeny, meany, miny, mo anthology. We didn't select what is here by taking it in turns to choose work we admired, but by collaboration. Every poem included in the book is here because more than two of us really wanted it to be.

The selection process became much more animated when it turned into an impromptu poetry reading, featuring the vocal skills of Carol Ann, Jean and William Sieghart. Reading poetry aloud invests it with an immediacy and force which solitary and silent reading misses. Public readings – in bookshops and pubs, libraries and theatres, as well as at literary festivals – are fast becoming a popular form of entertainment. Poetry is no longer the preserve of the high-minded lone reader, but a focus of lively, informal gatherings. The advent of National Poetry Day in October should help to spread this welcome trend, and to widen participation still further. Pablo Neruda filled football stadiums for his readings. In an age where television has replaced the hearth, it is good to see that the oral tradition is starting to flourish once again.

The Forward Book (and accompanying prizes) is drawn from poetry published in Britain over the past year. The work must be written in English, but that does not limit the geography of the poems: we looked at work from African, Canadian, Caribbean, Indian, Irish, New Zealand, Scottish and Welsh authors. And a wide mixture of cultural and ethnic interests were represented, which we have tried to reflect: all of the judges were sure that we did not want to produce what Jean called "another English literature" collection.

The forms of the poems, as well as their subject matter, remain as various as in previous years. No dominant style or school emerges. What links the work, as always, is the simple fact that most poets, most of the time, write about what matters most to them. Naturally enough, these tend to be the very things which matter to the rest of us: love and death; history and politics; places, people, ideas, God. It has been said that we read in order to know that we are not alone, in which case poetry offers the greatest sense of communion that we can find from words on a printed page.

Another gift of poetry is its ability to refresh jaded senses. A number of the poems here address the familiar in a delightfully unfamiliar way. Ancient myth and fairy stories attracted a lot of scrutiny this year, an interest which is also apparent in contemporary prose writing (if there is a movement afoot, it is this). Not all idols remained untoppled on their pedestals, but good poetry has always contained an element of the irreverent, if not the outright subversive. There are poems in this book about shops and singers (Bessie Smith, Marvin Gaye and Elvis all appear); about new neighbours and old lovers; about trout and moths and rivers and even, memorably, about a certain well-known newscaster. If some of these never seem quite the same again, this anthology will have been a success.

Cressida Connolly

Acknowledgements

Dannie Abse . CONDENSATION ON A WINDOWPANE . *On the Evening Road* . Hutchinson

Fergus Allen . ACTOR IN MIRROR . THE FALL . *The Brown Parrots of Providencia* .
  Faber and Faber

Moniza Alvi . THE SARI . *The Country at my Shoulder* . Oxford University Press

Eavan Boland . MOTHS . LOVE . *In a Time of Violence* . Carcanet Press

Dermot Bolger . WHEREVER YOU WOKE . *Soho Square* . Bloomsbury

Alan Brownjohn . BASTARD . *In the Cruel Arcade* . Sinclair-Stevenson

A.M. Budzisz . UNTITLED . *The Imam's Friday Sermon* . Janus

John Burnside . SEPTEMBER EVENING; DEER AT BIG BASIN . *The Myth of the Twin* .
  Jonathan Cape

Ciaran Carson . A DATE CALLED *EAT ME* . *First Language* . Gallery Press

George Charlton . IN THE CUL DE SAC OF MÉNAGE À TROIS . *City of Dog* . Bloodaxe Books

Brendan Cleary . CREEP . *The Irish Card* . Bloodaxe Books

Eleanor Cooke . MAN ON A BICYCLE . *Secret Files* . Jonathan Cape

Robert Crawford . THE NUMTIES . Poetry Review

David Dabydeen . EL DORADO . *Turner* . Jonathan Cape

Kwame Dawes . PROGENY OF AIR . NEW NEIGHBOURS . *Progeny of Air* . Peepal Tree Press

Peter Didsbury . A MALEDICTION . *That Old-Time Religion* . Bloodaxe Books

Helen Dunmore . THREE WAYS OF RECOVERING A BODY . *Recovering a Body* .
  Bloodaxe Books

Paul Durcan . PORTRAIT OF A YOUNG MAN . *Give Me Your Hand* . Macmillan

D.J. Enright . COMING TRUE . *Old Men and Comets* . Oxford University Press

Ruth Fainlight . CHOOSING . *This Time of Year* . Sinclair-Stevenson

Vicki Feaver . THE HANDLESS MAIDEN . NAKED GIRL WITH EGG . *The Handless Maiden* .
  Jonathan Cape

Padraic Fiacc . ENEMY ENCOUNTER . *Ruined Pages* . The Blackstaff Press

Roy Fisher . HYPNOPAEDIA . *Birmingham River* . Oxford University Press

Michael Foley . TALKING TO GOD ON THE NEW BRIDGE OVER THE FOYLE . *Insomnia in the
  afternoon* . The Blackstaff Press

Sam Gardiner . PROTESTANT WINDOWS . The Poetry Society

8

Jean Sprackland . DEADNETTLE . Smiths Knoll, No. 6

Anne Stevenson . POLITESSE . *Four and a Half Dancing Men* . Oxford University Press

Sue Stewart . HANSEL'S BIRTHDAY . *Inventing the Fishes* . Anvil Poetry Press

Gillian Stoneham . ELEPHANTS . The PHRAS 94 Open Poetry Competition Winner

Anthony Thwaite . FOR GEORGE MACBETH . *The Dust of the World* . Sinclair-Stevenson

Hugo Williams . JOY . *Dock Leaves* . Faber and Faber

Enda Wyley . BOOKS, POETRY IN THE MAKING . *Eating Baby Jesus* . Dedalus Press

Contents

The Best Collection Poems

Eavan Boland

[handwritten: THIS IS NOT A VERY GOOD THING.]

MOTHS

[handwritten: AT FIRST I TOOK IT FOR DECAY= BROWN SPOTS. BUT REF "MID-JULY" BELOW, I'M AFRAID HE MEANS "REDDEN". NVG.]

Tonight the air smells of cut grass. *[handwritten: OFTEN DOES, SO WHAT?]*
Apples rust on the branches. Already summer is
a place mislaid between expectation and memory. *[handwritten: THAT'S JUST AWFUL.]*

This has been a summer of moths. *[handwritten: OK, SO —?]*
Their moment of truth comes well after dark. *[handwritten: LAWKS! IMAGINE, MOTHS AFTER DARK]*
Then they reveal themselves at our window-
ledges and sills as a pinpoint. A glimmer.
[handwritten: NOT MUCH DIFF.   THEY/A   HACKNEYED UNACCELERATED   NO GOOD REASON FOR THIS LINE BREAK]
The books I look up about them are full of legends,
ghost-swift moths with their dancing assemblies at dusk.   *[handwritten: THIS ISN'T LEGEND — NATURE STUDY RATHER]*
Their courtship swarms. How some kinds may steer by the moon.
[handwritten: THIS IS GOOD; BUT THEN NOTHIN L]
The moon is up. The back windows are wide open.
Mid-July light fills the neighbourhood. I stand by the hedge.
[handwritten: — SINCE LAST SUMMER/LIGHT/NEVER — — WHAT?]

Once again they are near the windowsill – *[handwritten: WHY NOT JUST THE WINDOW]*
fluttering past the fuchsia and the lavender,   *[handwritten: (IF THE LAVENDER WERE WHITE OR RED OR YOUNG OR HIGHER OR WOULD IT WARN THEM?]*
which is knee-high, and too blue to warn them
[handwritten: THE MOON! THE KITCHEN BULB?]

they will fall down without knowing how
or why what they steered by became, suddenly,
what they crackled and burned around. They will perish-
[handwritten: AGAIN, NOT MUCH DIFF.]   *[handwritten: BULB DOES, MOMENTS DON'T HAVE LOBES ON TRAVERSALS LOS; THEY ARE (IF YOU MUST) TYPES-IDIOLS]*

I am perishing - on the edge and at the threshold of
the moment all nature fears and tends towards:
[handwritten: WHO SAYS IT?   BAD]

the stealing of the light. Ingenious facsimile. *[handwritten: WHAT IS AN INGENIOUS FACSIMILE OF WHAT]*

And the kitchen bulb which beckons them makes
my child's shadow longer than my own. *[handwritten: 1) HOW DOES THAT WORK! 2) LIFE = SHADOW? (TO COME)]*

[handwritten: WHY   " AND ",   —SIC, PLS.]

16

LOVE

Dark falls on this mid-western town
where we once lived when myths collided.
Dusk has hidden the bridge in the river
which slides and deepens
to become the water
the hero crossed on his way to hell.

Not far from here is our old apartment.
We had a kitchen and an Amish table.
We had a view. And we discovered there
love had the feather and muscle of wings
and had come to live with us,
a brother of fire and air.

We had two infant children one of whom
was touched by death in this town
and spared: and when the hero
was hailed by his comrades in hell
their mouths opened and their voices failed and
there is no knowing what they would have asked
about a life they had shared and lost.

I am your wife.
It was years ago.
Our child is healed. We love each other still.
Across our day-to-day and ordinary distances
we speak plainly. We hear each other clearly.

And yet I want to return to you
on the bridge of the Iowa river as you were,
with snow on the shoulders of your coat
and a car passing with its headlights on:

I see you as a hero in a text –
the image blazing and the edges gilded -

and I long to cry out the epic question
my dear companion:

Will we ever live so intensely again ?
Will love come to us again and be
so formidable at rest it offered us ascension
even to look at him ?

But the words are shadows and you cannot hear me.
You walk away and I cannot follow.

Vicki Feaver

THE HANDLESS MAIDEN *

When all the water had run from her mouth,
and I'd rubbed her arms and legs,
and chest and belly and back,
with clumps of dried moss;
and I'd put her to sleep in a nest of grass,
and spread her dripping clothes on a bush,
and held her again – her heat passing
into my breast and shoulder,
the breath I couldn't believe in
like a tickling feather on my neck,
I let myself cry. I cried for my hands
my father cut off; for the lumpy, itching scars
of my stumps; for the silver hands -
my husband gave me – that spun and wove
but had no feeling; and for my handless arms
that let my baby drop – unwinding
from the tight swaddling cloth
as I drank from the brimming river.
And I cried for my hands that sprouted
in the red-orange mud – the hands
that write this, grasping
her curled fists.

In Grimm's version of this story the woman's hands grow back because she's good for seven years. But in a Russian version they grow as she plunges her arms into a river to save her drowning baby.

Naked Girl With Egg
after Lucien Freud

While she discards coat, skirt,
cashmere sweater, a string of pearls,
and lies ready on the bed, left hand
propping her left breast, body twisted
into an S, he fries two eggs

and brings them in on a white dish.
Then he sets to work – his brush
slithering over lustrous flesh,
the coarse dark hair between her legs,
like a tongue seeking salt.

She keeps her mind fixed on the eggs,
as if by concentrating hard enough
she'll discover a meaning as obvious
as in one of those paintings
where a skull, bottom left, equals death.

What could be homelier, or more comforting,
than to dip toast soldiers
into soft yellow yolks? Yet she thinks
of a day on the moors when she trod
on a curlew's nest, and of herself

posed on the black coverlet
to satisfy something – still loose
in the world – that likes nothing better
than to be fed on a naked girl
with two fried eggs.

Kathleen Jamie

FOUNTAIN

What are we doing when we toss a coin,
just a 5p-piece into the shallow dish
of the fountain in the city-centre
shopping arcade? We look down
the hand-rail of the escalator
through two-three inches of water
at a scatter of coins: round, flat, worthless
reflections of perspex foliage
and a neon sign – FOUNTAIN.
So we glide from mezzanine to ground,
laden with prams, and bags printed
Athena, Argos, Olympus; thinking: now
in Arcadia est I'll besport myself
at the water's edge with kids,
coffee in a polystyrene cup.
We know it's all false: no artesian well
really leaps through strata
fathoms under *Man at C&A*, but
who these days can thrust her wrists
into a giggling hillside spring
above some ancient city?
So we flick in coins, show the children how:
make a wish! What for, in the shopping mall?
A wee stroke of luck? A something else, a nod
toward a goddess we almost sense
in the verdant plastic? Who says
we can't respond; don't still feel,
as it were, the dowser's twitch
up through the twin handles of the buggy.

Skeins o Geese

Skeins o geese write a word
across the sky. A word
struck lik a gong
afore I wis born.
The sky moves like cattle, lowin.

I'm as empty as stane, as fields
ploo'd but not sown, naked
an blin as a stane. Blin
tae the word, blin
tae a' soon but geese ca'ing.

Wire twists lik archaic script
roon a gate. The barbs
sign tae the wind as though
it was deef. The word whustles
ower high for ma senses. Awa.

No lik the past which lies
strewn aroun. Nor sudden death.
No like a lover we'll ken
an connect wi forever.
The hem of its goin drags across the sky.

Whit dae birds write on the dusk?
A word niver spoken or read.
The skeins turn hame,
on the wind's dumb moan, a soun,
maybe human, bereft.

Alan Jenkins

MISSING

Messages. The dumb machine's small bright red eye
is blinking on and off, and I'm home and dry –
the cat uncurls and looks up, stretching, yawning
in a wedge of light between the windowsill and broken
  blind,
the grey-blue light of five-thirty in the morning…
The blue light was my blues, the red light was my mind…
Another half an hour and the adult video begins
once more behind my bloodshot, sleepless eyes:
is it life-saving, wrestling? Everybody wins, she pushes him away
but only to clutch him closer, surprise, surprise,
no dream-stewardess is offering me coffee, though it's day
coming red-eyed over the roofs, over the rim
of the world, bringing for me cat's-breath, for her: him.

                                    *

Under-achieving, Underground-haunting, I descended to
a twilit flickering world, as I'd been led to expect;
I followed with my eyes the lighted windows rattling past
and found you out in one of them, moving too fast
for a sound to leave my open mouth. Could I detect
some sadness on your face, beautiful, downcast?
What assignation drew you on? There came a blast
of noise, a rush of foul air, a red light changed to green
somewhere far down the line, you did not look back,
and in your hurry to be moving you had not seen
how in another second you'd be changing track…
If you are Eurydice, could I be Orpheus, I mean
could anything I might still say or sing reclaim you?

                                    *

Return, re-run, a dream of moon-reflecting sea,
a neon beach-bar, teenage crowd and glowing jukebox,
the screen alive with ghosts, the comical dubbed voices
and the couples sitting, knees drawn up on the sand;

we are drifting away from them, close and slow,
not talking, arms around each other's shoulders lightly –
the whole day's heat has soaked into our itching backs…
We kiss, your tongue is warm and quick, but something stops you,
you break away and run towards the sea, you turn and
suddenly, remembering *It's not like years ago*
the fear of getting caught   the recklessness in water
a flash of white your little gasp and you are swimming brightly
away from me   the undertow *What if there were two*

*

Paris, and the boulevard I walked down with you
towards your mother's charming attic, your mother who
so charmingly stayed with friends while we played house
and fooled around; and here is the café where you sat
for you to take your picture, pouting *à la parisienne*;
here is the little bridge that crosses to the Ile St Louis
where you clutched me – though we were already late
for our rendezvous, for the movie, everything –
and opened your lips and said 'Kiss me! On ze mouse!';
here are the old men by their bookstalls, regarding me strangely
for here I am weeping, remembering *St Louis. Louis*, the Seine
cold-grey below, staring until one of them takes my arm
gently, and leads me nowhere, away from here, from harm.

*

Heroine of your teen romance, and so much a child
that when I called and found you swaddled on a sofa
in a kind of nappy (the 'thing' had split, you'd been emptied out
and the blood and after-pain were all you had to suffer)
you could smile at me, a dazed and happy smile
as I fed you cakes and poured champagne – sweet things…
We were celebrating, I was yours – why should you doubt? –
and had been since the night you shyly asked to stay,
unpeeled, unhooked, turned unhesitatingly
towards me, 'trembling with excitement' as you later said;
no thought for the thing flushed down, away,
no thought for the world that wasn't you and me,
no thought, now, for me (sweet things he told you 'turned your head').

You were quiet, in your bath, and you were going to sleep with him.
I knew it, the cat knew it. The bath-water felt it,
and the sliver of soap with which you soaped your quim,
the sponge with which you soaked your breasts, both smelt it –
when you clasped your nose and swiftly ducked
(sink or swim, you witch!) your hair waved like sea-grass,
your thatch, laid flat like tangled seaweed, foam-flecked,
lifted on the swell, and a slither of eel-slick skin
showed like the pearl-pink inside of a shell…
You surfaced, shifted slightly, settled your arse.
I saw it clenching tightly as his fingers gripped,
I saw your sea-anemone open, close as he plunged in.
Looking up, you smiled. I would say you slipped.

*

She moves on. She moves on,
taking with her when she's gone
your jacket, jeans and shirts,
your better self. It hurts and hurts.

She moves on. 'What this place needs',
she said when she first stayed the night,
'is a woman's touch.'
And she gave it that all right –
books trashed, clogged hairs in the sink;
she scarred your back, kneed you in the crotch,
told you that you stank of drink,
stabbed you in the heart. It bleeds and bleeds.

She moves on. Into another world,
one in which you don't belong
and one in which she never furled
her legs round yours, and the song
has changed, for ever, and is wrong:
not 'Marry me' or 'Let's do it'
but 'I want us to be friends.'
And you can see right through it,

and it claws and claws, and never ends.

She moves on. Now what she thinks
is that you didn't love her, not enough,
and that he's 'easy-going'. And it's tough,
your wanting her. It stinks.

She moves on. She doesn't call,
she won't come back, she's too far in,
her love was as fake as her leopardskin,
as quickly shed. You fall and fall.

She moves on. Like a single cell,
like a virus, with as much in mind,
as much concern for what it leaves behind,
as much speed. And it's hell, it's hell.

*

Missing, believed lost, five feet four–and–a–half
of warm girl, of freckled skin and sulky laugh
and blood on the sheets and ash on the pillow
with the smell of bacon eggs and lubricant – how that lingers –
for breakfast; crumpled things to scoop up from the floor and press
against my face, and cunt-smell on my fingers;
I'll skip the part about love it seems so silly and low
– the aftertaste of afternoons in a strange bed in a stranger's
flat, 'I love the way you go down on me', breathless, 'more.
Harder', and a red dress from the wardrobe, and the dangers:
at 3 a.m. your boot like a bad dream pounding on the door
and the way that anything you wanted could be true,
if you said it was. But not this. Missing. You.

*

Over. It's over. Three words uttered matter-of-factly
that I hear over and over in the sound of the wheels
hissing through rain, pointed north, as I drift in and of sleep
on the back seat, remembering our scenes, line by line, exactly
remembering line by line the words that tell you how it feels
to have brought this sadness with you from the womb

remembering *I could turn you inside out* on the car stereo
you swung like a handbag to our hotel room
and your body kneeling, bent double, face buried in the duvet,
 remembering how I stayed awake all night to watch you sleep,
lips parted, eyelids flickering *She is so beautiful she is so young
  and Oh*
our drive next day through driving rain, our bickering
I can't stand this, give me 'Les douleurs', give me Dufay

*

Viera Lodge: a drystone wall and one bent tree
and nothing else between us and the boiling sea,
the slate-grey, roiling sea. The wind wails
and we are safe inside, drinking, hearing how
a boy from the island, nineteen, hanged himself for love
of a girl up for the holidays from Glasgow.
And suddenly, for no reason, or for love,
I see myself walking down the slight slope of lawn
in the awful slate-grey light of dawn,
the cat prowling round an empty flat, listening for the key
in the lock, racing after shadows; red sails
in the sunset, a profile in the prow – it's you –
a world away from where I lie, bloated, blue.

*

Every move you make, every step you take – the 'disco-deck'
throbs, a blaze of glory as the evening flashes, fades;
waterlight flushes us, glass after glass brings back the blood
to day-defeated faces, each one doing its best
to hide a grey fatigue. You are not here, we flash and fade
as the loud, lit boat glides through London, I am obsessed –
in a small saloon, a scattering of couples watch the end
of *L'Atalante*, then *Ai No Corrida*, cries and whispers drowned
by the throbbing engine. You saw it with a girlfriend
and called to say, 'I need you, now. Can I come round?' –
I turned you away. My stomach churns, I turn and wade through dreck
of bodies – every vow you break, every smile you fake –
that twist and writhe in water, clutch and clasp in mud.

*

She came racing towards me, across a dancefloor
littered with tables, bottles, petals; she wore a flower
behind her ear, her hair piled high on her head,
wisps falling carelessly; my child-bride, my sweet
stamped her foot, one side then the other, flamenco-style,
gathered her skirt in both hands, by the hem,
and tugged it, left, right, in time with her stamping feet;
raced towards me, zig-zagged, in front of me, behind,
a challenge in her eyes and in her wide white smile…
It's crazy what you could have had, it's crazy what you could have had,
it seems a shame to waste your time to me – R.E.M.
remind me, I re-wind, replay, I know by heart
that was just a dream Pause Stop *I need this* Start

*

Now that I no longer sleep,
now I could no more count sheep
than the nights they spend together, or apart,
now I pray she'll have a heart
and come back, and come back,
now I stare into a black
and featureless night that goes on
and on, a grey and featureless dawn,
now that the telephone is quiet
and the memory runs riot,
now that I mix up the days
and am fuck-all use in several ways,
now that she's safely in the sack
with someone else, and won't come back,
now that I'm rotted through and stink
of loneliness, self-pity, drink,
now that she's finally taken off
and I'm left here to shake and cough
and wait for my first heart-attack
or for her to wake up and come back,
now that no-one wants to know
who I see, what I do or where I go,
now that more flee from me each week,

the women who sometime did me seek,
than I've had dinners on my plate,
now that her love has turned to hate
I think of this: the open-handed way I had
of slapping her, her lovely face, her head,
and making her see stars,
or pushing her downstairs
and out of the door. There's more –

*

Open me, the book says – *Cherokee*, by Jean Echenoz –
when I brush it, hunting up something else, and so I do,
and on the title-page, an entry-wound, black and yellow-brown,
the words 'Hole by Murphy, summer 1991' –
the ash dropped from your cigarette, your head dropped in a doze
to your chest, and the paper burned right through
to page thirteen; the sun in Brittany burned down,
your head jerked upright from its dream, your face was flushed
and freckled, your plump pale arms and shoulders turning red –
had your mother seen, your aunt seen? They went on sipping tea
and talking. Was it that day you wrote 'Nom d'une pipe,
tu me manques' and sent the postcard that flutters now from the book
you gave back sheepishly, unread? (Tearstains by Alan, 1993)

*

Night, the roof is leaking, and I perform my dance
with saucepan and bucket, and the steady drip, drip
of dirty water tells how love leaked out of my life;
for two years, I tried to stop the holes and fill the cracks
but there were always more, and the slow drip of slights,
insults, screaming on the telephone, hanks of hair
yanked out, left a stain that spread everywhere.
So now that the roof leaks, and the cat looks askance
at my attempts to catch as I would a second chance
these drops like huge tears falling from black heights,
I drink up regret, to the last drop,
and stop and let it all come down in cataracts
to drown me: night and rain and the thought of my not-wife.

Paul Muldoon

THE SONOGRAM

Only a few weeks ago, the sonogram of Jean's womb
resembled nothing so much
as a satellite-map of Ireland:

now the image
is so well-defined we can make out not only a hand
but a thumb;

on the road to Spiddal, a woman hitching a ride;
a gladiator in his net, passing judgement on the crowd.

Ovid: *Metamorphoses*
(*Book VI, Lines 313-81*)

All the more reason, then, that men and women
should go in fear of Leto, their vengeful, vindictive numen,
and worship the mother of Apollo and Artemis
all the more zealously. This last tale of the demise
of Niobe brought others to mind, inspiring no less zeal
among the storytellers. 'On the fertile soil
of Lycia,' one began, 'the peasants, too, would scorn
Leto and pay the price. Since these Lycians were low-born,
the remarkable story of what happened
is scarcely known, though I saw with my own eyes the pond
where the wonder took place. My father, being too frail
to travel far himself, had sent me on the trail
of a string of prime bullocks he'd turned out
in those distant parts. He'd given me a Lycian scout
whom I followed over the rich
pasture till we came on a lake in the midst of which
stood an ancient altar, its stones blackened
by many sacrificial fires, set in a quicken
of reeds. The scout stopped in his tracks and said in a quiet
voice, "Have mercy on us" and I echoed
him, "Have mercy". When I asked my guide
if this was a shrine to the Naiads or Faunus of some such god
he replied, "Not at all, son: no common hill-god or genius
presides over this place but the one whom Juno
sentenced to wander round and round,
never to set foot on solid ground;
the goddess who dwells
here was the one to whom even Delos
gave short shrift,
though Delos itself was totally adrift;
on that unstable island, braced between a palm and a gnarled
olive, she brought her twins into the world,
then, clasping them to her breast,
set off again with Juno in hot pursuit.

By the time she touched down in Lycia, the bailiwick
of the Chimera, she was completely whacked
from her long travail; the intense heat
had left her drained; her breast-milk had run out.
Just then she stumbled upon a fair-to-middling-sized pond
in which some locals were cutting osiers and bent
and sawgrass and sedge.
Leto knelt by the water's edge
and made to cup her hands. But these local yokels
shook their reaping-hooks and sickles
and wouldn't let her drink. 'Why,' she begged them, 'why
would you deny me what's not yours to deny
since water, along with air and light,
is held by all in common, as a common right?
It's not as if I'm about to throw
myself headlong into your pool. My throat's so dry
and my tongue so swollen I can barely utter
this simple request for a life–giving drink of water
If not for mine, then for my children's sakes,
I implore you to let us slake
our thirsts.' At that moment, the twins stretched
out their little hands. Who could fail to be touched
by such entreaties? These begrudgers, though, were moved
only to renew their threats and foul oaths:
then, to add insult
to injury, they began to stomp about and stir up the silt
on the bottom of the pond, muddying the water
out of no motive other than sheer spite.
That was it: that was as much as the Titan's daughter
could take; 'Since you've shown,' she cried, 'no soft spot
for me, in this soft spot you'll always stay.'
And stay they have: now they love nothing more than to play
in water, giving themselves over to total
immersion or contentedly skimming the surface; they dawdle
on the bank only to dive back in; now, as ever,
they work themselves into a lather
over some imagined slight; since they continually curse

and swear their voices are hoarse
while their necks, in so far as there's anything between
their heads and shoulders, are goitred; with their yellow
paunches set off by backs of olive-green,
they go leaping about the bog-hole with their frog-fellows." '

The Best First Collection Poems

Fergus Allen

ACTOR IN MIRROR

Dark roles, my agent says they're me -
Iago, Bosola, Thersites
And specimens of today's manhood
From similar stables, assorted
Pimps, betrayers and glassy psychopaths.
Not for me the bravura villain
Or cool-headed amorous spy,
Only the kind you want to spit on.

When it's *She Stoops* or *The Importance*
The phone is silent, I perform
Light housework for ladies and gentlemen,
Repolishing their polished floors,
Searching in their watery pier-glasses
For the devil-face in the window.
But the flesh-coloured moon looks harmless –
Innocent eyes estimating innocence.

Yes, I know there's a hint of shark
In the overshot jaw and gliding
Gait, but not in the mind's construction.
Visit the whitewashed cells inside:
No spiders crouching or moulds fruiting
On these hygienic walls; Charles Kingsley
Can take a guided tour – and leave
A water baby if he wishes.

The Fall

The Garden of Eden (described in the Bible)
Was Guinness's Brewery (mentioned by Joyce),
Where innocent Adam and Eve were created
And dwelt from necessity rather than choice;

For nothing existed but Guinness's Brewery,
Guinness's Brewery occupied all,
Guinness's Brewery everywhere, anywhere –
Woe that expulsion succeeded the Fall!

The ignorant pair were encouraged in drinking
Whatever they fancied whenever they could,
Except for the porter or stout which embodied
Delectable knowledge of Evil and Good.

In Guinness's Brewery, innocent, happy,
They tended the silos and coppers and vats,
They polished the engines and coopered the barrels
And even made pets of the Brewery rats.

One morning while Adam was brooding and brewing
It happened that Eve had gone off on her own,
When a serpent like ivy slid up to her softly
And murmured seductively, Are we alone?

O Eve, said the serpent, I beg you to sample
A bottle of Guinness's excellent stout,
Whose nutritive qualities no one can question
And stimulant properties no one can doubt;

It's tonic, enlivening, strengthening, heartening,
Loaded with vitamins, straight from the wood,
And further enriched with the not undesirable
Lucrative knowledge of Evil and Good.

So Eve was persuaded and Adam was tempted,
They fell and they drank and continued to drink
(Their singing and dancing and shouting and prancing
Prevented the serpent from sleeping a wink).

Alas, when the couple had finished a barrel
And swallowed the final informative drops,
They looked at each other and knew they were naked
And covered their intimate bodies with hops.

The anger and rage of the Lord were appalling,
He wrathfully cursed them for taking to drink
And hounded them out of the Brewery, followed
By beetles (magenta) and elephants (pink).

The crapulous couple emerged to discover
A universe full of diseases and crimes,
Where porter could only be purchased for money
In specified places at specified times.

And now in this world of confusion and error
Our only salvation and hope is to try
To threaten and bargain our way into Heaven
By drinking the heavenly Brewery dry.

Kwame Dawes

PROGENY OF AIR

The propellers undress the sea;
the pattern of foam like a broken zip
opening where the bow cuts the wave

and closing in its wake. The seals bark.
Gulls call and dive, then soar loaded with catch.
The smell of rotting salmon lingers over the Bay

of Fundy, like a mortuary's disinfected air;
fish farms litter the coastline;
metal islands cultivating with scientific

precision these grey-black, pink-fleshed fish.
In the old days, salmon would leap up the river to spawn,
journeying against the current. They are

travellers: When tucked too low searching for
undertows to rest upon, they often scrape
their bellies on the sharp adze and bleed.

Now watch them turn and turn
in the cages waiting for the feed of
colourised herring to spit from the silver

computer bins over the islands of sea farms,
and General, the hugest of the salmon,
has a square nose where a seal chewed

on a superfreeze winter night when
her blood panicked and almost froze.
Jean Pierre, the technician and sea-cage guard,

thinks they should roast the General in onions

and fresh sea water. It is hard to read mercy
in his stare and matter-of-factly way.

He wears layers, fisherman's uniform,
passed from generation to generation:
the plaid shirt, the stained yellow jacket,

the ripped olive-green boots, the black
slack trousers with holes, the whiskers
and eye of sparkle, as if salt-sea has crystallised

on his sharp cornea. He guides the boat in;
spills us out after our visit with a grunt and grin,
willing us to wet our sneakers at the water's

edge. The sun blazes through the chill.
The motor stutters, the sea parts, and
then zips shut and still.

Stunned by their own intake of poison,
the salmon turn belly up on the surface;
then sucked up by the plastic piscalator,

they plop limp and gasping in the sunlight.
One by one the gloved technicians
press with their thumbs the underside of the fish

spilling the eggs into tiny cups
destined for the hatchery, anaesthetised eyes
glazed shock on the steel deck.

They know the males from the females:
always keep them apart, never let seed touch egg,
never let the wind carry the smell of birthing

through the June air. Unburdened now the fish
are flung back in — they twitch, then tentative

as hungover denizens of nightmares, they swim

the old sisyphean orbit of their tiny cosmos.
The fish try to spawn at night
but only fart bubbles and herring.

On the beach the rank saltiness of murdered salmon
is thick in the air. Brown seaweed sucks up the blood.
The beach is a construction site of huge cement blocks

which moor the sea-cages when tossed eighty feet down.
They sink into the muddy floor of the bay and stick.
There is no way out of this prison for the salmon,

they spin and spin in the algae-green netting,
perpetually caught in limbo, waiting for years before
being drawn up and slaughtered, steaked and stewed.

And in the morning's silence,
the sun is turning over for a last doze,
and silver startles the placid ocean.

Against the grey green of Deer Island
a salmon leaps in a magical arc,
slaps the metal walkway in a bounce,

and then dives, cutting the chilled water on the other side.
Swimming, swimming is General (this is my fantasy)
with the square nose and skin gone pink with seal bites,

escaping from this wall of nets and weed.
General swims up river alone,
leaping the current with her empty womb,

leaping, still instinct, still travelling
to the edge of Lake Utopia, where
after so many journeyings, after abandoning

this secure world of spawning and living
at the delicate hands of technicians,
after denying herself social security and

the predictability of a steady feeding
and the safety from predator seal and osprey;
after enacting the sisyphean patterns of all fish,

here, in the shadow of the Connors Sardine Factory
she spawns her progeny of air and dies.

New Neighbours

and you know there is a path here
which you must find

somehow quietly
and when you find it

keep it to yourself
like a talisman

and simply toe
the line

don't
smudge it.

Lavinia Greenlaw

A Letter from Marie Curie

The girl dying in New Jersey
barely glances at the foreign words
but she likes the stamp.
It is a kind of pale blue
she hasn't seen much of.
The lawyer who brought the letter
talks of a famous scientist
who found the magic ingredient
that made the clockfaces she painted
shine in the dark. He doesn't say
that each lick of the brush
took a little more radium
into her bones, that in
sixteen hundred years
if anything remained of her
it would still be half as radioactive
as the girl is now,
thumbing through the atlas
she asked her sister to borrow.
He explains that Marie Curie
is anaemic too, but the girl
isn't listening. She's found France;
it's not so big. The lawyer shrugs:
She says to eat plenty of raw calves' liver.

ELECTRICITY

The night you called to tell me
that the unevenness between the days
is as simple as meeting or not meeting,
I was thinking about electricity –
how at no point on a circuit
can power diminish or accumulate,
how you also need a lack of balance
for energy to be released. *Trust it.*
Once, being held like that,
no edge, no end and no beginning,
I could not tell our actions apart:
if it was you who lifted my head to the light,
if it was I who said how much I wanted
to look at your face. *Your beautiful face.*

Conor O'Callaghan

MENGELE'S HOUSE

It was considered
the finest in its street
on the outskirts of Buenos Aires.
Splashing and screams were heard
during the long July heat
in adjacent gardens.

Nobody has lived there
since the last family fled.
Now and then a researcher comes,
or a would-be buyer
armed with rosary beads
noses around the bedrooms.

Since all the glass
was kicked from a window
by legless students,
the lambency of trees
is free to come and go
in the gutted kitchen.

Out the back are piles
of twigs and compost,
a seventies lawnmower
and aquamarine tiles,
exactly as they were left
by the last owner,

who talked about himself a lot,
chatting across the fence,
but never had the neighbours
past his gate,
and never even once

darkened their doors.

In the neighbourhood
he's remembered still.
He was the old misery
who had strange kids,
a swimming pool,
and a history.

RIVER AT NIGHT
for Vona

We do this at least once a year.
The midges, the cow parsley, the stagnant air

are signposts to the only deep enough pool
after weeks have dried the current to a trickle.

After too much heat, and too much cider,
the night seems forever and the water inviting.

We have walked for miles into unfenced land
where the hum of the distant town is drowned,

and find again that the core of summer
is cold against our sun-burned shoulders.

There's no special way of deciding who goes first.
It just happens that my jeans and tee-shirt

have been left on parched, hoof-marked earth
where a cigarette ripens closer to your mouth.

On the other bank, an orchard and the sky's
expanse spread out like a field of fireflies.

No birdsong, nothing swaying in the high grass,
and little that ties us to what we recognise.

The silence is only disturbed by your voice
saying it can't possibly be so easy,

the planets blossoming. Only the remote throng
of cars at closing time asks if this is wrong.

To forget ourselves and a world more sober.

To forget that the slow persistence of the river

among black horses, black ragwort, black crab-apple trees
is just the brief eternity between two boundaries.

That when we walk this way in a different year
the same sense of longing will still be here.

On the surface of the universe my splashing
and your laughter scarcely make an impression.

After the silence has resumed you say that at some
point we should think of turning back. Come.

For now the night is shining in your arms
Imagine that we've shaken off the sun and its harness.

Take off your bracelet and your black dress,
and stretch out across the confluence of two days

to where I am floating in darkness.

The Best Single Poems

Robert Crawford

THE NUMTIES

The parsnip Numties: I was a teenager then,
Collecting clip-together models
Of historical windsocks, dancing the Cumbernauld bump.

Satirical pornography, plant-staplers, nostalgiaform shoes
Were brochure-fresh. It was numty-four
I first saw a neighbour laughing in a herbal shirt.

Moshtensky, Garvin, Manda Sharry –
Names as quintessentially Numties
As Hearers and Bonders, duckponding, or getting a job

In eradication. Everything so familiar and sandwiched
Between the pre-Numties and the debouche of decades after.
I keep plunging down to the wreck

Of the submerged Numties, every year
Bringing back something jubilantly pristine,
Deeper drowned, clutching my breath.

M.R. Peacocke

TANGO

Let us invent marble and five o'clock.
I'll take white, you take black.
How engagingly we rhyme
across the chequered level in the perfume
of tea and petits fours.

I shall sample the tiniest slice
of the Grand Succès on the lemon terrace,
the newly apparent moon
a delicacy cat-ice thin,
fresh as mimosa.

Your legs are dangerously long
under the palm trees at Menton,
my thighs all silk and hesitation
drawing the tango down
the polished length of the floor.

And the cellos have such slim waists
and violins are girls with flattened breasts.
Let us invent the chaise longue,
bamboo, Lapsang Souchong,
linen and panama.

You may cough and thump your stick,
but I have been up in the attic
and I have a bundle of postcards here to prove
that once we were seen to be in love
on the Riviera in nineteen twenty four.

Robin Robertson

THE FLAYING OF MARSYAS
nec quicquam nisi vulnus erat (Ovid, *Metamorphoses*, VI, 388)
I

A bright clearing. Sun among the leaves,
sifting down to dapple the soft ground, and rest
a gilded bar against the muted flanks of trees.
In the glittering green light the glade
listens in and breathes.

A wooden pail; some pegs, a coil of wire;
a bundle of steel flensing knives.

Spreadeagled between two pines,
hooked at each hoof to the higher branches,
tied to the root by the hands, flagged
as his own white cross,
the satyr Marsyas hangs.

Three stand as honour guard:
two apprentices, one butcher.

II

Let's have a look at you, then.
Bit scrawny for a satyr,
all skin and whipcord, is it?
Soon find out.
So, think you can turn up with your stag-bones
and outplay Lord Apollo?
This'll learn you. Fleece the fucker.
Sternum to groin.
Tickle does it? Fucking bastard,
coming down here with your dirty ways...
Armpit to wrist, both sides.

Chasing our women . . .
Fine cuts round hoof and hand and neck.
Can't even speak the language proper.
Transverse from umbilicus to iliac crest,
half-circling the waist.
Jesus. You fucking stink, you do.
Hock to groin, groin to hock.
That's your inside leg done:
no more rutting for you, cunt.

Now. One of you each side.
Blade along the bone, find the tendon,
nick it and peel, nice and slow.
A bit of shirt-lifting, now, to purge him,
pull his wool over his eyes
and show him Lord Apollo's rapture;
pelt on one tree, him on another:
the inner man revealed.

III

Red Marsyas. Marsyas *écorché,*
splayed, shucked of his skin
in a tug and rift of tissue;
his birthday suit sloughed
the way a sodden overcoat is eased
off the shoulders and dumped.
All memories of a carnal life
lifted like a bad tattoo,
live bark from the vascular tree:
raw Marsyas unsheathed.

Or dragged from his own wreckage
dressed in red ropes
that plait and twine his trunk
and limbs into true definition,
he assumes the flexed pose of the hero:

the straps and buckles of ligament
glisten and tick on the sculpture
of Marsyas, muscle-man.
Mr Universe displays the map of his body:
the bulbs of high ground carved
by the curve of gully and canal,
the tributaries tight as ivy or the livid vine,
and everywhere, the purling flux of blood
in the land and the swirl of it flooding away.

Or this: the shambles of Marsyas.
The dark chest meat marbled with yellow fat,
his heart like an animal breathing
in its milky envelope,
the viscera a well-packed suitcase
of chitterlings and palpitating tripe.
A man dismantled, a tatterdemalion
torn to steak and rind,
a disappointing pentimento
or the toy that can't be reassembled
by the boy Apollo, raptor, vivisector.

The sail of stretched skin thrills and snaps
in the same breeze that makes his nerves
fire, his bare lungs scream.
Stripped of himself and from his twin:
the stiffening scab and the sticky wound.

Marsyas the martyr, a god's fetish,
hangs from the tree like bad fruit.

Iain Crichton Smith

AUTUMN

The boy in brown school uniform is munching an apple.
The air is beginning to grow cold on the teeth.

In the bare fields, there are barrel-shaped strawy bales,
and a buzzard rests comfortably on a fence post.

Time to assess, facing the bathroom mirror in the morning,
while the vague steam wreathes around you.

Time to remember those you have betrayed,
those who are waiting to write your history.

The young boy riding the tractor plays pop music:
the hills are upside down in calm lochs.

She passes your window again, the girl with the two black dogs
who are dragging her eagerly towards the village.

Will you watch the minister chatting at the church door
in his black cloak, finished with the sermon.

Eat your strawberries, and consider the rowan tree
which reflects serenely from the ballads.

My hypocrisies, when shall I be rid of them,
when shall I stand up bare of rustling leaves

and their endless intricate gossip. The day passes
with its pictures across your retina

and the whiskery drunkard holds out his hand.
The unemployed man asks if he can clear your rones.

At the Book Night we read Wilkie Collins
and think of sentimental Victorian autumns.

In the hospital the old lady does not recognise you.
The old man wishes to be taken fishing.

The nurses all in white are at their vigilant tasks,
the vases are filled with autumn flowers.

Do you wish to visit Venice or Florence,
to hang up paintings in the banal day.

Splendid frosty stars. The owl and the mouse.
The scholar studying an anthology.

Someone is burning papers in a late field.
The orphan sparks drift out of darkness.

The weight of the past descends on the shoulders of statues.
How many did I forget in order to climb my mountain

so as to be at last finished in flawless marble.
My youth how thoughtless, my middle age how busy,

and my old age hawk like but powerless.
So much I might have done but didn't,

so much I did that was egotistical.
The diamond sparkles from the aged hand

I can hear the frost blooming slowly on water.
My shoe creaks and creaks on its surface.

An old teacher sits quietly in a Home
diligently marking his register

while all around him are shadows of quadrilaterals.

The unmarried matron is white as snow.

Pull your coat tightly about you,
tighten your belt and your vain desires.

Keep them on a leash as you walk your dog
through the housing scheme in the evening.

Profound crown of the year, time of memory,
souvenirs of travels, of successes, failures.

The cards are placed on the table once again,
kings and queens and the sunny-faced jokers,

and the diamonds you never had, and the elegiac spades,
and the hearts which are burning like sunsets.

Oaks, forgive us, and the orange-coloured beeches,
we are heavy with a strange pregnancy,

with beginnings and endings all at once.
Bitter-sweet autumn, remember our crimes

and do not judge us. Lead us onward
to a chaste winter and then a fertile spring

where the waters break freely like our tears
and the laughter and weeping are sparkling,

as the hand turns over a new page
scrabbling like a squirrel in the midst of plenty.

Autumn is necessary as spring,
as the glowing helmets of summer.

It is a time of rummaging through attics.
of archaic brown, hue of the pilgrim's cloak.

it is the time of luxurious melancholy,
of a splendid sunset which you do not deserve,

of a safe though inadequate pension.
Tell me, Hugh, are you here again,

I remember you from the school and the factory.
How many cars we assembled together

that we could not buy, those Rolls Royces
sliding smoothly up secret drives.

Let all be swept away. Bring on winter.
Let the agonising portraits be expunged

and let us have fresh windy galleries.
Absolve us, Nemo. Let the deer step out

gracefully and daintily. Reflect,
creative nurseries, your brilliance.

Forget, forget, let us begin again,
address unruefully our envelopes

to the major world, the fresh and haggard strangers
who tell us tales of the astonishing stones.

Gillian Stoneham

ELEPHANTS

"Elephants," he shouted,
"elephants!"
from his small, bare room with the window open
on the second floor;
shouted because
elephants were what he had most wanted
all his life to see.
Neighbours and people
in the opposite street, paused
in a rattle-tattle of washing up and being busy,
to glance out of the summer-day window, paused
in their important
discussion of politics in the sitting room and
their tending of potatoes in the back garden,
and said "<u>That</u>
is the old man shouting again."
And his relatives
interrupted their thoughts for just a moment
to sigh with resignation.
But no-one attempted to go and look
in the small square room
where the old man sat on the edge of his bed
smiling and satisfied,
as the elephants, ponderous but gentle
walked round and round, snuffing the air
with their curious trunks, and treading
ever so softly.

The Other Poems

Dannie Abse

CONDENSATION ON A WINDOWPANE

1

I want to write something simple,
something simple, few adjectives,
ambiguities disallowed.

Something old-fashioned:
a story of Time perhaps
or, more daringly, of love.

I want to write something simple
that everyone can understand,
something simple as pure water.

But pure water
is H_2O
and that's complicated
like steam, like ice, like clouds.

2

My finger squeaks on glass.
I write JOAN
I write DANNIE.
Imagine! I'm a love-struck
youth again.

I want to say something
without ambiguity.
Imagine! me, old-age pensioner
wants to say something
to do with love and Time,
love that's simple as water.

But long ago we learnt
water is complicated,
is H_2O, is ice, is steam, is cloud.

Our names on the window
begin to fade.
Slowly, slowly.
They weep as they vanish.

Moniza Alvi

THE SARI

Inside my mother
I peered through a glass porthole.
The world beyond was hot and brown.

They were all looking in on me—
Father, Grandmother,
the cook's boy, the sweeper-girl,
the bullock with the sharp
shoulderblades,
the local politicians.

My English grandmother
took a telescope
and gazed across continents.

All the people unravelled a sari.
It stretched from Lahore to Hyderabad,
wavered across the Arabian Sea,
shot through with stars,
fluttering with sparrows and quails.
They threaded it with roads,
undulations of land.

Eventually
they wrapped and wrapped me in it
whispering *Your body is your country*.

Dermot Bolger

WHEREVER YOU WOKE

There only ever was one street,
    One back garden, one bedroom:
Wherever you woke you woke beneath

    The ceiling where you were born,
For the briefest unconscious second
    An eyelid's flutter from home.

Alan Brownjohn

BASTARD

Into a suddenly sunny spring dawn
A bastard creeps out through a crack in some
Until-then immaculate-looking woodwork.

He inhales the air and smiles, and everything
Looks good to him. And so he takes a few
Experimental paces, trying out

His legs and wondering what clothes to wear:
A city suit? Some jeans and a baseball cap?
Or an 'I ❤ my building society' T-shirt?

Because he plans to walk into an Organisation,
To stir things up inside an Organisation.
He is going to Go For It and get others Going,

And he's past Reception already, and up
In an express lift to a penthouse suite already,
And they have an office waiting for him already,

And his first dictated letters on a screen.
In the other offices, behind their hands,
They are talking about him, quite a lot,

They are saying, 'How did that bastard get that job?
I'd like to know where the hell he came from!
I'd like to see his qualifications for doing

What he does.' – All talk, and he knows it, it's safer
To talk than to act, the smaller bastards
Know the truth of that from long experience,

They've learnt to carry on and keep their heads down

To protect their own bit of woodwork. So all goes well,
With the faxes slithering out from other bastards

In other penthouse suites all round the world,
And the graph turning upwards on the wall-chart in
The Bastard's Conference Room, the spread-sheets glowing

With the marvellous figures the Bastard envisages;
And his desk is clear and shiny, and people's smiles
Are amiable and innocent, or seem so.

Or seem so...In his deep suspicious brain
The Bastard worries occasionally that their lips
May be smiling, smiling for him, but not their eyes.

Still, for now, things go splendidly, the Bastard is seen
On 'State of the Art' and 'Man of the Week', and has
A 'Room of my Own' and a 'Holiday of my Choice'.

- And then one day a casual conversation
Stops short when he enters a room without warning
And another day the people do not stop

When he comes round the door, but self-consciously keep talking
With knowing looks, and ever-widening smiles.
The Bastard pretends he hasn't noticed, but

He goes back to his office and he thinks
'Those bastards could be ganging up on me...
I must watch that little bastard with the haircut.'

The Bastard is full of fear and fantasy,
And the fantasy that made his world for him
Becomes a fantastic fear of losing it:

His mirror tells him always to guard his flanks,
And never leave his knife-drawer open when

He turns his back on even his secretary

-But he does have courage. It tells him to have it out
Face-to-face with his team of Assistant Bastards
And find out what the hell is going on.

Oh no, they'll never tell him half the story,
Oh yes, they'll sit and talk behind their hands,
But he can still fire the lot; or he thinks he can.

Today they are gathered round a table, with vellum pads
Which some of them are writing or doodling on,
And some are self-confidently leaving quite untouched.

It's the ones who pick up no pencils and take no
Notes who are the most dangerous. They know
The result they want without fidgeting about it;

Especially the little bastard with the haircut.
He speaks in code but it's clear what he's implying:
The Bastard is letting the Organisation down,

It ought to do better; and all the smallest bastards,
The shareholders' democracy, have been stirred
To demand a different bastard at the top.

This year they're eager for a different scene,
This year they're after a man with a different style,
This year they'd like a bastard with a haircut.

The Bastard's hand is turning clammy on
His thoroughly doodled vellum pad,
The sky is blue for other bastards now.

He sees what is coming next, and he'll speak out first.
He rises from the table, he looks at them
With steady eyes, and steady eyes look back,

Though the lips are smiling. 'I've seen your game!' he shouts,
'I've sussed it out – you're just a lot of *bastards*,
A lot of dirty, crooked, scheming *bastards*!'

When the door slams hard behind him they look at each other
And shake their heads with humane and pitying smiles.
'Poor bastard,' one compassionately murmurs.

The haircut says, 'It wasn't easy, but
It had to be.' And a third: 'I'm so relieved
It's over and we can breathe.' And a grinning fourth

In a flak jacket moves into the Bastard's chair
As the sun sets golden, and the immaculate walls
Begin to look like very porous woodwork.

A.M. Budzisz

Poor Mohammed,

Jesus Christ
super-starred in
a grand
rock opera

but you appear
in banned novels
and rejected poems.

John Burnside

SEPTEMBER EVENING; DEER AT BIG BASIN

When they talk about angels in books
I think what they mean is this sudden
arrival: this gift of an alien country
we guessed all along,

and how these deer are moving in the dark,
bound to the silence, finding our scent in their way
and making us strange, making us all that we are
in the fall of the light,

as if we had entered the myth
of one who is risen, and one who is left behind
in the gap that remains,

a story that gives us the questions we wanted to ask,
and a sense of our presence as creatures,
about to be touched.

Ciaran Carson

A Date Called *Eat Me*

The American Fruit Company had genetically engineered a new variety
    of designer apple,
Nameless as yet, which explored the various Platonic ideals of the
    'apple' synapse.

Outside the greengrocer's lighted awning it is dusky Hallowe'en. It is
Snowing on a box of green apples, crinkly falling on the tissue paper.
    It is

Melting on the green, unbitten, glistening apples, attracted by their
    gravity.
I yawned my teeth and bit into the dark, mnemonic cavity.

That apple-box was my first book-case. I covered it in wood-grain
    Fablon —
You know that Sixties stick-on plastic stuff? I thought it looked
    dead-on:

Blue Pelicans and orange Penguins, *The Pocket Oxford English
    Dictionary*;
Holmes and Poe, *The Universe*, the fading aura of an apple named
    Discovery —

I tried to extricate its itsy-bitsy tick of rind between one tooth and
    another tooth,
The way you try to winkle out the 'facts' between one truth and
    another truth.

Try to imagine the apple talking to you, tempting you like something
    out of Aesop,
Clenched about its navel like a fist or face, all pith and pips and sap
Or millions of them, hailing from the heavens, going *pom, pom, pom,
    pom, pom*

On the roof of the American Fruit Company, whose computer banks
   are going *ohm* and *om*.

They were trying to get down to the nitty-gritty, sixty-four-thousand
   dollar question of whether the stalk
Is apple or branch or what. The programme was stuck.

The juice of it explodes against the roof and tongue, the cheek of it.
I lied about the *Fablon*, by the way. It was really midnight black with
   stars on it.

George Charlton

IN THE CUL DE SAC OF MÉNAGE À TROIS

Your house – it's sad, this kitchen dim,
Spirits that inhabit here
Indifferent, or else outdoors,
And the atmos – *ugh!*- the atmosphere

Is something else: an odour
Of damp clothes, the washing-machine
Defending its corner, inert,
Resentful of a sudsy routine.

At least, seemingly, you please
The fridge, offering propitiously
A bottle, a milky appeasement,
Accepted apparently.

Yet its flex, a tendrilled ivy,
Is tightening its grip, machismo
As your husband – your husband
Of whom you have said: 'Like so

Much make-believe he cannot
Be believed.' As he has said, often:
'It's difficult not to think of a wife
And at the same time another woman.'

And this while your young son slept on
In his dream of bad monsters.
And to think, at a takeaway, once,
Two drunks mistook us for lovers.

Brendan Cleary

CREEP

Judith was just 16
I was 43

what an endeavour
talking to her
about pop music
turned out to be

I'm a bit creepy

that's what I heard
her whispering
to her mates

'he's a bit creepy'...

Eleanor Cooke

MAN ON A BICYCLE

The bees settle on the keystone.
The swarm seethes. A man pedals
into the courtyard – the temple garden
fills with students on bicycles.

The professor tells them that the bees
are exactly where he said. 'They dance
for me,' he cries, 'and only I
can tell precisely where they'll go.'

The queen detaches herself from the swarm,
lines up the professor's prick
and stings him through his lederhosen.
He leaps into the air, spiralling,

pedalling. Dancing for the bees.
The bicycle watches, calculates
his exact angle to the sun,
and sails riderless into the sky.

David Dabydeen

El Dorado

Juncha slowly dying of jaundice
Or yellow fever or blight or jumbie or neighbour's spite,
No one knows why he turns the colour of cane.

Small boys come to peep, wondering
At the hush of the death-hut
Until their mothers bawl them out.

Skin flaking like goldleaf
Casts a halo round his bed.
He goes out in a puff of gold dust.

Bathed like a newborn child by the women.
Laid out in his hammock in the yard.
Put out to feel the last sun.

They bury him like treasure,
The coolie who worked two shillings all day
But kept his value from the overseer.

Peter Didsbury

A MALEDICTION

Spawn of a profligate hog.
May the hand of your self-abuse
be afflicted by a palsy.
May an Order in Council
deprive you of a testicle.
May your teeth be rubbed with turds
by a faceless thing from Grimsby.
May your past begin to remind you
of an ancient butter paper
found lying behind a fridge.
May the evil odour of an elderly male camel
fed since birth on buckets of egg mayonnaise
enter your garden and shrivel up all your plants.
May all reflective surfaces
henceforth teach you to shudder.
And may you thus be deprived
of the pleasures of walking by water.
And may you grow even fatter.
And may you, moreover, develop athlete's foot.
May your friends cease to excuse you,
your wife augment the thicket of horns on your brow,
and even your enemies weary of malediction.
May your girth already gross
embark on a final exponential increase.
And at the last may your body, in bursting,
make your name live for ever,
an unparalleled warning to children.

Helen Dunmore

THREE WAYS OF RECOVERING A BODY

By chance I was alone in my bed the morning
I woke to find my body had gone.
It had been coming. I'd cut off my hair in sections
so each of you would have something to remember,
then my nails worked loose from their beds
 of oystery flesh. Who was it got them?
One night I slipped out of my skin. It lolloped
hooked to my heels, hurting. I had to spray on
more scent so you could find me in the dark,
I was going so fast. One of you begged for my ears
because you could hear the sea in them.

First I planned to steal myself back. I was a mist
on thighs, belly and hips. I'd slept with so many men.
I was with you in the ash-haunted stations of Poland,
I was with you on that grey plaza in Berlin
while you wolfed three doughnuts without stopping,
thinking yourself alone. Soon I recovered my lips
by waiting behind the mirror while you shaved.
You pouted. I peeled away kisses like wax
no longer warm to the touch. Then I flew off.

Next I decided to become a virgin. Without a body
it was easy to make up a new story. In seven years
every invisible cell would be renewed
and none of them would have touched any of you.
I went to a cold lake, to a grey-lichened island,
I was gold in the wallet of the water.
I was known to the inhabitants, who were in love
with the coveted whisper of my virginity:
all too soon they were bringing me coffee and perfume,
cash under stones. I could really do something for them.

Thirdly I tried marriage to a good husband
who knew my past but forgave it. I believed in the power
of his penis to smoke out all those men
so that bit by bit my body service would resume,
although for a while I'd be the one woman in the world
who was only present in the smile of her vagina.
He stroked the air where I might have been.
I turned to the mirror and saw mist gather
as if someone lived in the glass. Recovering
I breathed to myself, *'Hold on! I'm coming.'*

Paul Durcan

Portrait of a Young Man

If we all of us had a choice of our own death
- And I see no reason why we should not –
I would choose to be murdered by a woman.

I am a man for all mothers.
A woman with whom I'd have slept
Billions of times.

Not with a boning knife. I do not
Like knives, cannot bear the sight of knives.
No. I would like her to smother me with a pillow

Without warning in the middle of a love bout
At the top of her bed, at the height of her passion
To bring the pillow down on my face and I drown

In its ice-blue linen but not before
I put up a stiff resistance, making her
Cry out my name above the traffic and the owls.

It will be twilight in early June mist.
Life is a process of illuminating
A moment to accommodate the inspiration.

D.J. Enright

Clichés (how one used to despise them!) are coming true. The sun rises, and the sun goes down. There is a season for everything; also for nothing. The knees tremble; desire falters (except for a quiet drink). The grinders aren't what they were (they were never much). Can't see too well; soon there will be an end to the reading of books. Nor hear: the daughters of music are brought low on Radio 3. You look on your labour, and mostly it's vanity or vexation. There is no remembrance of things past. Fears are in the street. Jugs and cups get broken. No doubt crickets would be a pest, were there any left. Yes, the words of the wise (God damn them) are like nails. One nail drives out another. So find some better clichés.

Ruth Fainlight

CHOOSING

How I yearned for a velvet dress
with a shirred waist and lace collar
like all my friends, but couldn't choose
which colour - dull green or
lurid red. It seemed a contest
between the nursery horrors
of a fairy-story forest
and the scary glamour
of portentous tomorrows – crazy
guesses and conjurations based on
grown-ups' talk, books and movies.

There is a photo of me
in a garment almost the pattern
of that ideal model.
Above the collar, a self-conscious
face, tormented by the problem
of choice – and every other
(which from the vantage of the present
moment, still make me want
to laugh or weep or fight).
So was it red, green or blue
I chose? I – or my mother.

Padraic Fiacc

ENEMY ENCOUNTER

Dumping (left over from the autumn)
Dead leaves, near a culvert
I come on
      a British Army soldier
With a rifle and a radio
Perched hiding. He has red hair.

He is young enough to be my weenie
- bopper daughter's boyfriend.
He is like a lonely little winter robin.

We are that close to each other, I
Can nearly hear his heart beating.

I say something bland to make him grin,
But his glass eyes look past my side
- whiskers down
                the Shore Road street.
I am an Irish man
             and he is afraid
That I have come to kill him.

Roy Fisher

HYPNOPAEDIA

As I expounded *The Man With the Blue Guitar*
my students outwitted me.

Eyes glazed, or averted, they declined
to pick up a single question,
forcing me to drone on alone. I was so boring
I fell asleep.

Then a little way off
through the opaque white screens in my head
I started to make out a voice.
It was expounding *The Man With the Blue Guitar*.

Startled, I awoke, talking. Seven stanzas it had taught
without any prompting from me. Though curious,
I still didn't have enough gall
to check its performance from anybody's notes.

Michael Foley

TALKING TO GOD ON THE NEW BRIDGE OVER THE FOYLE

The best you could expect would be an answering machine:
God is attending a seminar on The Management of Change.
But to talk to the Void isn't strange. I've often prayed to stars
The distant, deaf and *non-existent* screen stars:
Marlon, share your deep power with me. Teach me to brood.
Forgive the familiar tone, Lord. I can't believe in a distant God
Who uses us for some higher purpose we can't understand
Transcendental because of a black balaclava, saying:
'This is beyond you. You'll just have to suffer. Tough turd.'
So it's casual thanks for your gifts – for Manhattan, Montmartre
And the new bridge over the Foyle that sings perpetually in the wind
Attracting a film crew in search of 'the positive aspects of Ulster life'.
I feel Godlike myself at the top of the great central span.
All you Prods to the east bank, to Deanfield, Rossbay,
                           Cedar Manor, Dunwood.
Reap your just rewards, My Chosen Ones. This Land is Your Land.
From the Waterfoot Inn to Larne Car Ferry and from Ballygawley
                           to the Giant's Causeway
Business shall flourish with the words of Isaiah on the front of the till
And no waves but in Lisnagelvin Leisure Centre new children's pool.
You Fenians, stay west in Gleneagles, Ashgrove, Baronscourt,
                           Hampstead Park.
Run up your velvet curtains there. Cast off. Lie back.
Propitious winds bear you off forever from the three-foot men
Upstream where the smoke from slacked parlour fires drifts on the
                                town
And 'the boys' fight for liberty – ('Don't do what *they* tell you.
Do what *we* tell you.') Stronger the scouring wind. Sing, bridge,
                           and fly
Your own flag – a jazzy red-and-white-striped wind sock that rides
                           high in
Untrammelled exultant wind running like beasts major corporations use
                           in their ads

The big lithe loping cats and svelte galloping thoroughbreds tossing
their manes.
Massive underfoot throb – like a great ship. Touch the rail – you feel
the singing pulse.
Extravagance and hope fill my heart. *Perhaps I won't die in Derry on a*
rainy day.
Behind me Lough Foyle and the sea, on the east the North on the west
the South
Where the statutes are frozen in stone but the statues move
And thousands churn fields to mud hoping for visions of sweet-natured
virgins.
What appears in most fields are new Tudor-style homes.
Pass on, weary traveller. Bright shine the carriage lamps, sweet sound
the chimes
But they'll bring you contempt and fury framed in wrought-iron perms.
Here on wooded banks aluminium-framed picture windows catch light
To make the tops of the top nested coffee tables gleam.
Money talks – wheedles, shouts, swears – but affects a sacred hush at
home.
Inward inward the gaze, blind the windows that stare on each side.
Lord, we're labelled and frozen like rich men's sperm.
Flesh is weak – and the spirit is weaker still.
Needing hard mind soft heart we loll hard of heart soft in the head.
Though we're subtle as Jesuits still when we justify.
Eastern wisdom I call my sloth and quietude.
Let the young curl their lips in contempt and my name
Be struck from the list of candidates for existential sainthood.
Lord, hear my sins. I speak as a weak man among weak men
With a heart like a deep-frozen haggis and a memory like Kurt
Waldheim.
I want to live. I want to feel. Hear me. Vouchsafe a sign.
Let me believe and care. Show me the wounds. Unclog my brain.
It's hard to remember here Your Beloved Son was a thinking man
Not the simpering half-gaga passive Sacred Heart on walls
But the fierce intense Jewish intellectual Pasolini showed
Striding up stony paths flinging truths over his shoulder
To willing but thick-headed followers stumbling behind.

Behold – a man who came not to reassure but disturb.
Awake, Fenians and Prods, from the shagpile dream of The Beeches
Heathfield, Summerhill, Meadowbank, Nelson Drive and Foyle
                                                    Springs.
Come in, Daisy Hill and Mount Pleasant. Do you read me, Dunvale?
Drive if you must but leave your steamed-up cars at the picnic spots
(One at each end, the Fenian side with no rusting chassis dumped yet)
And climb to the high bracing air where great truths are revealed.
Stand above and between, look down, across and then behind
Where the untroubled Foyle spreads out grandly, inexorably.
Button car coats and ponder. The drumbeat is lost on the wind.
The blood thicker than water dissolves in the sea.
At least the vista should inspire you to country-style song:
From the Lovely Hill of Corrody to the Point of Sweet Culmore.
Sing too, new bridge – though not of what's past or passing or to come
Just the one-note song that sometimes you sing so hard in the wind
The newly social-conscious RUC have to come and close you down.
No cars stop. No one comes. Too far for the three-foot men to walk
And too many career paths here for those who want to feel Supreme.
Also it's cold. Your whole face goes numb. Who can linger on heights?
Alone, you feel more like a crank. Now the traffic grows – *both ways.*
Not a change of heart – change of shift at the chemical plant
Du Pont, just in sight to the east, seven pillars of economic wisdom
Propping up a dour sky. 'How do you find the Yanks anyway?'
'Miserable shower a shitehawks.' Yet the cars pour out eastward
Glad of the work. More leisurely the homecoming line on this side.
A typical day's freight – the sullen, the weary, the compromised.
Just a bridge, not a symbol of hope – though it sings in the wind.

Sam Gardiner

PROTESTANT WINDOWS

They come at sunset peddling daylight, two
Salesmen wearing glasses, through which they view
His shabby sliding sashes with disdain.
"Wood?" they suppose and feign
Dismay. "Yes, comes from trees,"
And he raises the drawbridge ten degrees,
A hurdle to reservists
But child's play to front line evangelists
With news of paradise
On earth (at this address to be precise)
In whitest white PVC.
   "Think of all
The blessings. And if economical
Heavenly comfort isn't what you need
Think of Our Earth," they plead,
And their plastic-rimmed, double, glazed eyes glow
With love for generations of window
Salesmen as yet unborn. "If I were you,
I'd save my CO_2
For atheists and papists. I doubt
They even know about
King Billy." "Who?" William III to you,
Brought sliding sashes to
Britain, fetched in pure air and sanity.
Without him we'd still be
In the dark."
    "Sorry, we must go. It's late,"
They say, and beat a retreat to the gate,
And pause. Quick as a flash
He raises an effortlessly sliding sash
For a parting shot. "Plastic heretics!"
He shouts. The window sticks.
He tugs, a sash-cord snaps, the window drops

On his head, where it stops.
Latimer and Ridley know how he feels
As bloodied, martyred for his faith, he reels
Towards eternity,
Where planets, the latest novelty,
Are looking less and less
Like being a success.

Chris Greenhalgh

FROM As a Matter of Fact *(PART 1)*

The man sitting next to me on the plane
claimed
he'd collected one sachet of sugar
from every airline in the world.

He insisted on shaking my hand and
calling me repeatedly by my first name.
He probably has many friends and lots of money
and, feeling that exaggerated sense of mortality

you get at thirty thousand feet
and with the urge, correspondingly
strong, to relate my life-story to a stranger,
I said "no shit!" and noted parenthetically

that I had every backnumber of <u>Yeasty Catgirls</u>
ever printed, not to mention a few never
generally released. He countered with "the fact" that
he could fold a piece of paper

in half nine times. I said I'd once eaten
a whole jar of Cayenne pepper.
He rejoined that if I studied Figures 3,
7, 16 and 21 in some noted medical

encyclopaedia I'd see that the model
was him. He asked me what I did for
a living and I told him I counted cars
on a raised footbridge of the Holland Tunnel,

but that I used to be a lexicographer
with special responsibility for the letter F;
that was after I'd been a synopsiser

of detective novels. He said

he'd once appeared on CNN as a quote death-
threat recipient unquote and, as I expressed my
surprise, hostesses in British Airways livery
hovered with the suavity

of café violinists, deploying contoured
plastic laptop trays
of food on every table. Outside, the sky
griddled to pink and grey.

Geoff Hattersley

REMEMBERING DENNIS'S EYES

He always blinked too much,
like an overnight guest who leaves
with the toilet paper in his holdall
or leaves a dry blanket
covering a wet bed.
Even with the balaclava
turned round to hide his face
I could see him blinking
through the makeshift eyeholes.

Gimme the bastard bag
he yelled, tugging at it.
The iron bar bounced on
the guard's helmet five times
before he fell to his knees,
another four or five before
he lost his grip on the bag.
You saw nowt, *nowt*, Dennis hissed,
pinning me to the wall
with one hand, waving the bar
like a conductor with the other.

The last time I saw him,
years later, years ago,
he'd just tried to kill his ex-wife,
had been stopped by
his ten year-old daughter.
He was running toward Darfield
like a wind-up toy
with a pair of kitchen scissors
sticking between his shoulder-blades.

Stuart Henson

The Price

Sometimes it catches when the fumes rise up
among the throbbing lights of cars, or as
you look away to dodge eye-contact with
your own reflection in the carriage-glass;
or in a waiting-room a face reminds you
that the colour supplements have lied
and some have pleasure and some pay the price.
Then all the small securities you built
about your house, your desk, your calendar
are blown like straws; and momentarily,
as if a scent of ivy or the earth
had opened up a childhood door, you pause,
to take the measure of what might have been
against the kind of life you settled for.

Michael Hofmann

MARVIN GAYE

He added the final 'e'
to counteract the imputation of homosexuality.
His father was plain Revd Gay, his son Marvin III.

He slept with his first hooker
in the army, coming off saltpetre.
He thought there was another word for 'virgin' that wasn't 'eunuch'.

Including duets, he had fifty-five chart entries.
His life followed the rhythm of albums and tours.
He had a 'couple of periods of longevity with a woman'.

He preached sex to the cream suits,
the halter tops and the drug-induced personality disorders.
When his hair receded, he grew a woolly hat and beard.

Success was the mother of eccentricity and withdrawal.
In Ostend he felt the eyes of the Belgians on him,
in Topanga someone cut the throats of his two Great Danes.

At forty-four, back in his parents' house,
any one of a number of Marvins might come downstairs.
A dog collar shot a purple dressing-gown, twice.

Michael Horovitz

AFTER BROWNING

Summer's done
Birds in their heaven

All's well with the worm.

Louise Hudson

IT HELPS

They said you must talk to someone
so she talked
and talked
about the children,
schools, clothes,
about the house, garden,
car.
She talked and talked
on telephones, in pubs,
at restaurants
she'd entertain them all
with stories too scandalous
hilarious with the sound
of all those words.
She'd chat at the shops
discuss the weather, pass the time
of day, whisper about things
the children shouldn't hear;
like miscarriages, abortions,
sex or money.
At parties she could talk herself
to bed with men
make out she enjoyed it
liked them as they were.

Some nights she walked
around the house
just talking
the television murmured
upstairs the children
stirred in sleep.

It only took a split second

to slit her wrist
lengthways along the arm
they said "we didn't know
she should have said".

Colin Jack

The Loss of Chalmers' Memorial Church, Anstruther

A fisherman was first to see the fire.
A cousin of the family, lifting his lobster creels
At midnight. The blaze, he said, burned a pathway
To his boat, as if a finger stirred the flames
Spreading them down across the water.
Before the stone was cold, the black ruin
Was demolished, piece by piece. I missed it all
By just a week, but the town is still in shock.
The church, of course, was derelict already
There being less need than in my father's day.
I noticed, each time I returned, how much worse
The place was looking. They say that gypsies
Had been living there, and had started the fire;
That one had roasted to death, like a hedgehog
Cooked in clay, but no one can be sure.
Now it's gone, and the skyline over Anstruther
Looks different; the town has lost its shape, somehow.

By the water, I meet an old fisherman. He asks
About my father. *Not good. Another operation.*
They are taking him apart, I joke, bit by bit.
Tell him I was asking after him. More than ever,
This year, I feel his absence from these narrow streets.

They took the spire down slowly, slate by slate.
So a space which has been filled for years
Is returned to nothing and the empty sky.
The locals, having cast away the building
Are finding meaning in the stones, gathering them
For their gardens and their guilt.

In the boot of my car, I have a charred fragment
Of the pulpit, and a piece of red stained glass.

Jackie Kay

BLUES

Hell, I can't even take my own advice,
that's what she thought often, when her left eye
(always the left) was swollen and a blue river
ran underneath the brown; or when,
whole parts of her body could not
be walked on, or swam in, or touched even.
When her body had no-go areas; something-only areas.
Danger: a fence right round her skin, wooden
as her own voice the morning after

all that violence. It was in the way they looked at her.
It was not in her mind. She did not grow such looks
in her own backyard. The hard stare; the furtive one where
the eyes were a fast car swerving as she walked near.
Nothing could persuade her not to be funny.
She could not stop being funny. Making people
laugh till they cried, hurt themselves, howl.
She was a shouter. She could barrelhouse.
But on the morning after all that violence

she could not raise the roof of her voice.
She could not embellish or endow or growl.
Laugh, yes. Grunt. Giggle. Once she caught herself
in the trembling mirror. *A minstrel.*
She tried to be completely still.
As if she were committing a murder.
A clown. An aunt jemima. She has a smile
that could cross a river. And she had a laugh
that could build a raft. And that was all she had.

Frank Kuppner

FROM LAST ETERNAL MOMENTS *(SECTION 76)*

Some think God tortures us because he loves us so much.
What a shame he does not hate us, and treat us kindly.
Thus: every evening, regularly, for six or seven years,
The inoffensive and devout middle-aged woman
Lights a candle in front of a favoured religious image,
And prays intently. I do not know what for,
But it was not for this. One night, the candle
Catches the hem of her highly flammable nightdress,
Envelops her in flames, and burns her to death.
Thus she is taken off to meet her God of Love,
Possibly with a ready question on her lips.
Let us hope he was wearing some means of identification.
He could so easily be mistaken for his opposite number
By anyone who judges character in the light of actions.

Peter Levi

The full season comes to rest at high tide
when the wild sorrel rusts on the roadside,
it is a road you have often taken
or like a place long known, long forgotten:
under the rough fingers of chestnut trees
or where the wood squanders its mysteries.
Words finish, though the closing notes drag on,
I live among things past their true season:
God has crumbled the stars in his own sky,
nothing is breathing but antiquity,
our world is broken, it lies where it fell,
under the crust earth is an iron bell
heaving its awful weight around the sky:
it is swinging and clanging silently.
I say your likeness is to an old stone:
upright, raineaten, mooneaten, alone.

Edward Mackinnon

(EINDHOVEN, NETHERLANDS)

ALMOST LIKE JOE MEEK'S BLUES

It was in those days after Holly and the music died, when pop
was in a slump. He contrived to get songs that were crap to the top
of the charts. His name was in *Melody Maker* nearly every week
and it seemed to me in my grammar school days as though Joe Meek
produced every other hit. I pictured him raking in the lolly,
a sharp lad on the make, living it up in London, with a dolly
bird on each arm. But like fluff blown off a stylus he disappeared
without a trace. In any case, the music business was now geared
to a new sound: the Beatles and the Stones. Pop started to boom again.
I was going up to Cambridge. The swinging sixties could now begin.

He blew his brains out while I was there. But at the time I never read
the half-column on the inside page. I found out long after he was dead
that Joe was no flash Harry, but a slightly gauche and moody queer
who had been twiddling knobs since boyhood, an ace recording
                                        engineer
who spoke in soft Cambridgeshire tones and lived in a modest pad
in Holloway where he built his studio. People thought him half-mad
as he trailed microphone cables to the bathroom, but this was the
                                        ground
on which he waged his private battle, creating his own distinctive sound
and taking on Tin Pan Alley. He won and lost. They were unforgiving.
Working with show biz pseuds must have been even worse than living

in Cambridge, where as a pimply youth in incongruous black gown
I played at being an undergrad, and the grey streets of the town
brooded like the Bergman films I went to see, and girls were rare.
But he was more of a misfit than me, for he had no-one to share
and sustain that dream from which all pop music starts. I had the luck
to have friends to help me survive the Cambridge blues, and so I stuck
it out and got my degree. All he had was a lonely pride

in what he had achieved. In the end there was nowhere to hide after being found guilty of importuning. He died of shame. Poor Joe was queer, not gay. The swinging sixties never came.

E.A. Markham

DEATH IN THE FAMILY, 1988
after a father, for a mother

1
thinking about my mother, thinking
about a joke she might have told, setting
the scene to make it seem

unforced . . . The butcher's shop in Ladbroke Grove in the 50s
was a tough audition for one
unaccustomed to playing the messenger, or head of the family:

there, weighing need and status –
heads and tails and innards ruled out;
dead flesh to be cleaned ruled out –

bits of chicken, then, one bit for each member
for this is England and exile made you measure
not only the weight of glances and words thrown across the street

but what you ate
and how much warmth you let into the air around you:
five bits of chicken, please.

The telephone rang and rang and guilty
to be caught at this after 30 years
I learnt of a death in the family.

I listened to what accompanies news of death in the family,
and promised to pass it on,
and agreed how it should be passed on

And I checked myself for signs of afterlife.
The bath this morning to greet the world
seemed right; panic about bills unpaid began to subside.

The damp-marks in my room still sent the same message. REPAIR ME
Estrangement from a too-dear friend, her beauty flawed
in wanting to embrace the cheat in you –

seems less like logic now, less
like damp marks on walls, less like
your shift within the world.

For now, my son, a quiet hand has removed
a shelter that was useful, that was kind (why
aren't there hurricanes, revolutions, strange happenings as in *Lear*?)

There is nothing between you and the last appeal:
you are pressed against the barricades; the space
which cushioned till today, is occupied by you now:

you can't decline it, choice remains
but like a shadow to your *self*
like the two-headed coin you toss without protest: you must take

the weight of others
who will not grant breathing space
who look at you as fixture, always there

who are impatient, reckless, sporadic in their need
who want sometimes to fail – to check if you are real
who do and do not wish to take your place

and I go to the bathroom and find that things work much the same
and I suspect countries on the map are where we left them
and I welcome the shy, unexpected, prod of hunger . . .

2
I think back to that 50s scene
the lady (wife, long-distanced, to the one
whose death is now reported: we will tell her, we've discussed it)

losing her tongue, like a novice, at this butcher's shrine
(she knew a husband's commandments would be obeyed).
Later, it was possible, when chicken came in bits –

not that they came in bits, you understand: that was
the joke that never worked – later, in another part of town
when she had grown attuned to shopping

(but not to taking insides from dead meat)
she developed ways of withstanding
the pressure of the queue – and of honing her joke.

Five pieces not because there were five in the family
- there were five in the family –
but because in this England you had to count things differently.

From this they understood much
that she had not intended:
even the jokes here set you back.

Another failure, the family, growing tired of wings
made their own jokes of being tired of wings:
five *legs* seemed so difficult to be at ease with . . .

Thinking back to what produced five legs
she saw two of her mother's chickens *and a half.*
The horror of the half made her think

in this long-frozen land
where the family, itself a half of something never planned,
this was a joke all would understand:

so she asked for *five* pieces from two chickens
and a lame one; and the man with blood on him laughed
When she moved house again the other man laughed.

Chris McCully

WHITE TROUT
  for Owen Jacob

I wade out again into the dark water.
Where the blurred moon also rises
in her night metal I stem the river
and silently fish, grey as thought.

Hardly sight helps, only exploring
the line's curve under the fingers,
each draw, each slack of current weighing
differently, strange, remote.

But others move. The deeps liquefy
around them in their pause upriver –
one, ten, twenty or more of them
circling, then resting; all white trout.

There the fly is, double-hooked, a deft
mesh of feathers a bare foot down,
slowly arriving, slowly disappearing
as those sea eyes know it; as I know it.

And silently, fish run into the future,
slip the ripple into the stiller water,
finding smooth stone, the June dark,
the cast lighting on the moon's stunned arc.

Ian McDonald

Song in San Fernando

There was a silver girl sang in the streets
Sang in the old streets old and silver songs
The tamarind leaves fell like green wings as she sang
And the mountain men came to the black cobbled streets.

* * * *

Her hair was drenched with white scent
her face was pale as white candles in a church
Ah, her mouth was like a small fish gulping snow
All her clothes were silver English shillings.

* * * *

The mountain men big and black as rocks
They came from hunting birds green in the leaves
And gathered near the silver girl in seriousness
And heard song-sadness old as the policy of God.

* * * *

It was the song of death they loved, they remembered:
Who has touched the red berries of my breast and raped my daughters,
Put down my sons, sent donkeys into the shrines?
Despair engraved of the darkness after time has ended.

* * * *

It was the song of hunting they loved, they remembered:
The swords swung through pear boughs in preparation,
Used on wild hogs in the gold-bellied cassia forests,
On bright adversaries in man's imperilled future.

* * * *

It was the song of lust they loved, they remembered:
The women whom they met in golden creeks
Breasts to move the fingers over like rough brown silk
And warm bellies on the beds of dark-leaved corn.

* * * *

It was the song of youth they loved, they remembered:
Entrancement long as one star-dappled night
Ending quick beneath old suns and suffering
Blood burning old in sweet castles of the flesh.

* * * *

There was a silver girl sang in the streets
Sang in the old streets old and silver songs
All sadness were her old songs under every moon
Time bittered them always with the end of worlds.

Peter Redgrove

Eight Parents

I

At the climax of the illuminated
Book of Hours the Trinity is seen in truth to be
Three self-same white-clad bearded figures
Of Jesus on three identical thrones.
It makes the eyes go funny, like trifocals.

II

This devotional picture resembles
My mother's triptych dressing-table mirror;
When she sat there, three other mothers appeared.

III

The fourth turned round to me and smiled;
The three simultaneously looked back over their shoulders
At somebody out of sight down the glass corridors.
Then she got up, and the thrones were empty.

IV

Nearly a decade after she had emptied her throne, my father
Sat himself down in front of the same mirror and died.
He paid his Access- and paper-bill, laid out
Like hands of cards folders on the dining-room table
For his executors, climbed the stairs to his widower bedroom,
Sat down at my mother's mirror and saw there were three more of him,
Then his heart burst and shot him into mirror-land.

V

Where is that mirror now? you may be reasonably sure

If you buy a second-hand house or bed, then
Somebody has died in it.

VI

But a dressing-table triple mirror? Can you
Enquire of the vendor, expecting nothing but the truth
'Who died in this mirror?' Death
Leaves no mark on the glass.

Nicky Rice

THE AILING AUNTS

There were three of them, making it easier
for us to mock. The Three Weird Sisters,
we called them, or the Greek Chorus,
something at any rate dire and sonorous.

They were always checking each other's pulses,
ransacking cupboards for a thermometer,
disappearing under towels in a frenzy of Friar's
Balsam, or doing breathing exercises noisily.

They had hearts, arthritis, sensitive digestions
and various non-specific allergies
and they dined out on their 'ops' for years,
for ill-health was something to be cultivated,

providing it was neither wet nor smelly. It
suggested constitutional fragility like rare
porcelain. (Health was rude, opened its bowels
with clockwork regularity and sweated after exercise.)

They wouldn't make old bones, they said, hadn't
the stamina. There were references to terminal
conditions. They envisaged dying heroically, hands
limp, complexion fever-bright against starched linen.

In the end they never had to cope with cancer
or colostomy, or learn that illness could be
messy, needing its dressings changed.
They were lucky, I suppose, spent their last

days in geriatric wards where appearances didn't
matter and they developed enormous appetites,
wore awful dresses from a common pool

and wet their knickers when they felt like it,

and there were no deathbed leavetakings.
They died undramatically, too far gone
to exploit the possibilities,
wasting the opportunity of a lifetime.

Ann Sansom

VOICE

Call, by all means, but just once
don't use the *broken heart again* voice;
the *I'm sick to death of life and women
and romance* voice *but with a little help
I'll try to struggle on* voice

Spare me the promise and the curse
voice, the ansafoney *Call me, please
when you get in* voice, the *nobody knows
the trouble I've seen* voice; the *I'd value
your advice* voice.

I want the how it was voice;
the *call me irresponsible but aren't I nice* voice;
the *such a bastard but I warn them in advance* voice.
The *We all have weaknesses
and mine is being wicked* voice

the *life's short and wasting time's
the only vice* voice, the *stay in touch,
but out of reach* voice. I want to hear
the *things it's better not to broach* voice
the *things it's wiser not to voice* voice.

Peter Sansom

Today We Are Shooting Poets

not bad or good poets
not metrical, not free verse not concrete
or performance poets,
not poets who write about nothing but poetry and poets

not confessional poets,
English but like pop groups singing in American,

not poets writing as if they were talking as if
anyone ever talked like that,

not poets who write about what it is
never to be able to write, or love poems
or sex poems or poems about the colour of
their oppression or about the gender
of their oppression or about its class,

not poets with words all
over the place and lowercase i's,
not incomprehensible even to themselves poets

not poets who get famous for something
be it poetry or who they are or what they do
besides writing poems

not neglected poets
nor the experts on their own poems
who read nobody for fear of influence,

not poets up to the ears in scholarship
and not a spark in them

no. We are shooting the other poets.

You know who they are and I do.
Let's go buddy, let's do it.

Ken Smith

LOVESONG FOR KATE ADIE

Wherever it's bad news is where she's from –
a bronze leathery sort of lady, dressed for disaster's season,
a tough mouth woman, and like me a nighthawk. Ah, Katie,

reporting from the barbed wire rims of hell,
Katie at the barricades I dream of nightly, her voice
a bell in the desert wind, her hair blown which way.

It's true she loves it out where the disputed air
is vicious with shrapnel, bullet stung, the night's
quick stink of sulphur, flies, dead camels, terror.

But I don't mind now if she never comes back to me,
so long as she's happy. The night in her is enough,
that long-ago voice sets my gonads galloping.

Sure I'm afraid for her and pray every evening at 6
for her flight to some quiet place, cool nights
and nightingales between earthquakes and insurrections.

There we meet again, the night bright with stars:
Plough, Pleiades, Pole Star. She drinks, laughs
her special laugh, turns to go. We fall into bed.

We fuck all night, Katie & me, I never flag,
she never wearies, we're drunk on whisky and each other
and sweet fresh rocky and who cares it's Thursday?

She's there for me. I'm here for her. Any day of the week.

Jean Sprackland

DEADNETTLE

Sprawled under the hedge he snaps
the thin necks of deadnettle,
pinches the white sac, squirts
nectar into my mouth.
A small sweet promise on the tongue.

I run home in the heat. The smell
of melting tar, a stickiness underfoot.
The house whirrs and stutters with the machine.
She urges a small red dress to the needle.

She stops, examines me, stretches
to tug a snag of stickybud from my hair.
Be a good girl. She takes up the cloth

and snaps the thread on her teeth. *Won't you ?*

Anne Stevenson

POLITESSE

A memory kissed my mind
  and its courtesy hurt me.
On an ancient immaculate lawn
  in an English county
you declared love, but from *politesse*
  didn't inform me
that the fine hairs shadowing my lip
  were a charge against me.

Your hair was gods' gold, curled,
  and your cricketer's body
tanned—as mine never would tan—
  when we conquered Italy
in an Austin Seven convertible,
  nineteen thirty;
I remember its frangible spokes
  and the way you taught me

to pluck my unsightly moustache
  with a tool you bought me.
I bought us a sapphire, flawed,
  (though you did repay me)
from a thief on the Ponte Vecchio.
  Good breeding made me
share the new tent with Aileen
  while you and Hartley,

in the leaky, unpatchable other,
  were dampened nightly.
If I weren't *virgo intacta*,
  you told me sternly,
you'd take me like a cat in heat
  and never respect me.

That was something I thought about
   constantly, deeply,

in the summer of '54, when I
   fell completely
for a Milanese I only met once
   while tangoing, tipsy,
on an outdoor moon-lit dance-floor.
   I swear you lost me
when he laid light fingers on my lips
   and then, cat-like, kissed me.

Sue Stewart

Hansel's Birthday

Restless in the night, I find you harking back
to the old days of making do, on the hoof.
Dawn is a hunter and you run the gamut,
a fawn who limps his arrowed dream to my lap.

If I told you I'd baked a cake you'd mimic
the lake's transparent smile, make castles vanish
in mid-air like sand running free, running out,
and relive the barley-sugar's matchless kiss.

You were happier then, with berry and shrub,
chafing the plaited rushes of your lead.
Or piping the witch's tune, her five-mile step
no match for my stillness, the coiled entrapment

of a rose. Were we children when I, as swan,
skated the surface of your spilt mind's eye?
Now your fingers dislodge a pebble as white
as a moon or scout's palm your crumbs flew from

and I wear red to match the florist's bundle,
tempting you nearer the party by tugging
your voluminous sleeve, adopted sister,
familiar wife, as full of love as ever.

Anthony Thwaite

FOR GEORGE MACBETH

Wasted away –
Limbs, speech, and breath –
Such mockery, such sprightly gay
Spirits smothered, friend
Stubborn to call it death.
Make it all end.

Last words are right:
You whispered them
That last intolerable night,
Darkness itself, deep
Gathering of choked phlegm –
'How long will I sleep?'

Hugo Williams

Joy

Not so much a sting
as a faint burn

not so much a pain
as the memory of pain

the memory of tears
flowing freely down cheeks

in a sort of joy
that there was nothing

worse in all the world
than stinging nettle stings

and nothing better
than cool dock leaves.

Enda Wyley

BOOKS, POETRY IN THE MAKING

My father always kept his books clean.
When reading, he balanced those precious words
on his table of well-ironed corduroy thighs
and advised that like him I be careful to touch
with two fingers (quite briefly)
only the corners of each finished page
when ready to move on –
though often I would watch his hand
slowly feel across the turning thoughts,
like a man's light touch in reluctant farewell
of a face he has come to love.

Mine were the new but battered ones,
covers bent far back, edges creased.
"It's beyond me how you can manage
to mangle everyone", he'd taunt –
but I was finding in each mauled book
a home for my own ways; I liked sand
shifting where the pages joined in story,
breadcrumbs long left over
suddenly flaking free from words,
and split hairs forked above lines
as a diviner's stock over water –
all meant more than any signature to me,
that these books were mine.

Mine, marked with breakfast coffee spilt
on the earliest 50A ride to work,
the back seat windows
my jolting, smogged up pillows
while words unstuck the sleep in my eyes.

He sat with his books in our sitting room –

one finger pressed each line to life
while his tongue between teeth
wet his upper lip.

Closed, he marked them
with old card greetings
or writings from St. John
he'd discovered that February
early in his fortieth year.
He never drank or smoked again
but he still takes Marx down
from his full book shelf
arranged in Library order.
He was ever suspicious and knew
which ones had gone missing,
borrowed when I hoped he wasn't looking.

Just when he had no need to worry,
he chose my leave of home
to hide the books
behind his wardrobe door – the titles
like his absent daughter's name
he could never say again
without remembering too much.
Father, we will meet, surprised, someday,
both reaching for the same line.